AF485108

100 SENRYU AGAINST WW3

Chryssa Velissariou

100 SENRYU
AGAINST WW3

2022

Cyberwit.net

HIG 45 Kaushambi Kunj, Kalindipuram

Allahabad - 211011 (U.P.) India

http://www.cyberwit.net

Tel: +(91) 9415091004

E-mail: info@cyberwit.net

Printed at VCORRE PRESS.

Chryssa Velissariou

Dedicated to my family and to my second family, the fellow poets of the National Beat Poetry Foundation, Inc.

100 SENRYU AGAINST WW3

Chryssa Velissariou

INSTEAD OF A FOREWORD

There is no greater honor for the author of this book than to share her emotions with her fellow artists through her poetry and to experience their subtle souls' replies. I'm grateful to the incredible artists who read my poems and offered me a review about the book, as well as their thoughts on its theme: WAR. Let us hope that by working together, we will raise tremendous awareness about the Ukrainian War, which is in truth an unofficial third World War.

> **Deborah Tosun Kilday, Owner/CEO National Beat Poetry Foundation, Inc. USA**

There is no Peace in War. It is a silence, but not the meditative kind. It is a reminder that death will take you if you choose violence.

Instead, the guns must stay silent, there is another way. Using our voices for discussions, can bring cooperation and understanding.

Why is there war, and no peace? Have we ever had peace? The answers seem to reflect both. Peace, love and money are reasons used to start a war, but the reality is only death, debt, and sadness all come as a result of it.

War is not a good way to end conflicts. All that is left from war are the dead bodies of soldiers, orphaned children, and widowed wives.

Education is the key to end all conflicts. By educating people to understand that they must use their voices instead of guns, we can bring understanding that we

all have the same needs as our neighbors. The guns can be replaced by knowledge and books. Art can provide understanding and acceptance of our differences. Diversity can make us see our similarities and provide growth. War ruins our chances for good food, clean water, and a place to live.

Chryssa Velissariou, Greece International Beat Poet Laureate, gives you all the reasons in her book, "100 SENRYU AGAINST WW3".

With Peace, Love, Education

> **Ariadne Sawyer, CEO World Poetry Canada and International**

I am honored to write a comment on the dedicated peace activist Chryssa Velissariou and World Poetry Canada International Peace Ambassador. She inspires the world with her fine upcoming book, 100 Senryu Against WW3 and spreads much needed awareness for peace. She is a wonderful example of poetry and peace in deed and in spirit.

> **Ron Whitehead, U.S. National Beat Poet Laureate**

NO MORE WAR! Patriarchy Has Sown Destruction Long Enough! Women must have the same Rights as men! Freedom, Equality, and Justice are for ALL People! Democracy is for ALL People!

The time of the nurturing healing feminine energy has come. We must all, female and male, become healers. Peace love and understanding are not dirty weak words. Peace love and understanding are essential to our survival.

Chryssa Velissariou

Rather than viruses let us be healers, nurturers, gardeners dwelling harmoniously with each other, with Mother Earth.

Let us remember the heart. Let us practice resurrection.

These are the messages I receive from 100 SENRYU AGAINST WW3 by Greece's brilliant International Beat Poet Laureate Chryssa Velissariou! Her new book of poems and art is a treasure beyond measure.

> **Michael D. Amitin, NBPF International Beat Poet Laureate 2020, American poet and musician living in Paris, France.**

In this collection poet Chryssa Velissariou juxtaposes in words and drawings, the horrors of war with the beauty and innocence delivered in the natural world, and how anesthetized humans have become to wars fought in distant lands.

Left merely to flaunt slogans and meek protests as a narcotic to numb our hearts, we witness and are forced to accept war's barbaric annihilations as an ongoing, everyday occurrence.

Ms. Velissariou asks whether this can be considered civilization, as men who would gain from these heinous exercises continue to wield their greedy scepters.

Punctuated by clear, lovely drawings, this collection delivers a spacious and poignant meditation on the dark clouds hovering over our existence with this beautiful offering One Hundred Senryu Against WW3.

> **Jagjit Singh Zandu (Jit), M.Com., L.L.B., Author & Published poet, Reviewer, MOHALI, Punjab (India).**

Dr. Chryssa Velissariou of Larissa (Greece) has done an excellent job in creating "ONE HUNDRED SENRYU AGAINST WW3".

In this book, she describes the vulnerability of women and kids (due to exploitation at the hands of human traffickers) beautifully & vividly. They are left helpless and suffering victims of present-day war.

When I read through all her Senryu, I saw her sorrow for the refugees and the suffering humanity, while the executors, directors, and contractors of war only exploit the whole world by deriving benefits from the sales of guns and ammunition. She has beautifully painted war trade, losers, and gainers of the war.

I may not do her justice in such a short blurb. But I feel that she has expressed the war's torture almost in every aspect of human life especially women and kids that it's like she's putting the ocean into a bowl. This work of hers is really worth reading. I pray for success in her book.

> ➤ **Rtd Prof. Lathaprem Sakhya. Painter, poet and self-styled green woman, Kerala, India. She greens the earth by planting trees for the future generation**

The cover page tells it all. It has a picture of an owl and a phrase "Be Vigilant". The owl itself is a bundle of contradictions. And it is variously interpreted in various countries. But I feel, here the owl is a benevolent one. So, when you look at the cover, we realize that the book contains wisdom and knowledge as the owl is a symbol of both. The picture also urges one to think of a new beginning, a new way of life that puts an end to all war. And the Senryu are the poet's vociferous, lonely fight against war. And as the subtitle says it is also a warning to be vigilant against

war, as it can lead to the annihilation of this beautiful universe.

The book "100 Senryu Against WW3"is a heart wrenching appeal to the universe as a whole to stop fighting and think of peace. The poet artist has used her talents as a painter and poet to graphically describe the aftermath of war and what happens to the world if we, as humanity, do not start thinking of peace.

Each Senryu is a nugget of wisdom, urging the reader to go within himself and think of the various aspects of life, nature, animals, the universe, the people and the war which stands above it all as Damocles' sword. She has skillfully depicted in three economical, yet picturesque, speaking lines, how vigilant we, that is, the present humanity should be against igniting a third World War.

Like hordes of lonely fighters Velissariou has boldly made her protest against wars and the present war raging against Ukraine. She feels lonely in her fight, she says, but to me she is the very embodiment of courage. She has come forward boldly and impressed her convictions on war and how abhorrent it is for the whole of humanity and how important it is that we people of the world stand together for peace, to prevent the devastating Wars.

Borrowing David Thoreau' s words I describe Velissariou as a "one man majority" that is, she and her conscience against war is a majority that should be reckoned with. And her book is a bold and unique example of protest against war.

I too feel this universe and its people are too beautiful to be mindlessly destroyed by wars. Like Velissariou, I feel, we should all unite and work towards a universal

peace that would transcend all barriers and envisage the world as a huge single family as visualized in the

Indian concept of "Vasudhaiva kutumbakam" "The whole world is one family". This concept is derived from Maha Upanishad, an ancient Veda, in which we come across "ahimsa" or non- violence too, practiced both by Thoreau and Gandhiji as passive resistance and ahimsa respectively. This concept has to be inculcated and developed by each individual to ward off fights between human beings which in turn lead to wars and world wars. It urges us to rise above caste, creed, color and race and to love one another as we love ourselves.

> **Dr. Marieta Maglas, Poetess, Dentist, Paris, France (Romanian origin)**

The war is a metaphoric voice of the degraded human relations. This kind of degradation and dehumanization is the result of the contradiction between the nature of the war and the attainment of peace. The tendency of the developed societies was to become merged into a bigger one. When a nation causes worldwide mayhem with the purpose to pursue its idiosyncratic interest, this newly created chaos can destroy world solidarity and can affect the most important human right in life.

Even if the goal of the war is to maintain justice or to protect lives, it may mean evilness. We can see so many war clouds hanging over the inter-religious conflicts, over the colorism or shadeism, and over so many aspects of discrimination. How can we know for sure whether a war is holy or not?

I want to mention especially the crusades that have been in their beginning an expression of the Just-War Theory. People like Saint Augustine and Saint

Thomas formulated some religious criteria, more specifically, a legitimate authority must wage the war and morality has to be expressed in jus ad Bellum. Nowadays, the crusades do not need the army and I refer to the crusades against crime, vandalism, horrible animal living conditions, corruption, violence, abuse, absolutism, and intolerance.

As to the holy wars mentioned in the Old Testament, the New Testament advances from war of justice to love, forgiveness, and non-resistance for all the Christians that are the children of God. A war cannot be holy while taking human lives for whom Christ died. What frightens us is the idea of moving from conflict to war when pacifist methods are no longer effective.

Human perfectionism generated specific philosophical abstractions as the idea of the absolute war or ideal war, but unfortunately, they are not applicable in practice, so the only possibility to dominate the world is the total war with its specific purposes, methods, mobilization, and control. Total wars have occurred consistently throughout history.

God means love, justice, and mercy. Apostle Paul in Romans 13 clarifies the principle of justice:

"Everyone must submit himself to the governing authorities, for there is no authority except that which God has established. The authorities that exist have been established by God. Consequently, he who rebels against the authority is rebelling against what God has instituted, and those who do so will bring judgment on themselves." Paul believed that the ruling authorities are needed to maintain peace because the Lord is a God of order and not of chaos.

Examples of holy wars are the crusades that had been ordered by various popes between the eleventh and

thirteenth centuries. During the Crusades, the soldiers committed countless atrocities on behalf of God. Therefore, the concept of holy warfare has been lost in the Christian Churches.

The purpose of war is to restore justice when all peaceful alternatives have not worked out. The right purpose of war must be superior to its wrong cause.

In a war, the threatened nation needs war to restore justice and reduce needless deaths in the occupied territories. Pope Benedict XVI said that self-defense is a responsibility in the context of following Jesus who said, "Love your neighbor as you love yourself", Matthew 22:39. The most important demand is to love God, and this means to love His creation, the heaven, the earth, the plants, and the animals.

The war is evil because it flies in the face of nature. Troops move through the existing infrastructure in the wild and destroy the natural scenery. Land damage causes vegetation degradation over time.

For example, dry peat fire combined with rocket and artillery fire means toxic releases into the air. Oxides of sulfur and nitrogen can cause acid rain and soil acidification can cause the burning of vegetation, and conifers. Toxic substances enter the ground and can drift to groundwater. Petroleum products interfere with marine biocenosis. Some important birds require peace to procreate. War zones can disrupt them and cause exhaustion due to re-routing.

We need to breathe fresh air and drink clean water and only nature provides the essentials, it is our life-support system. The point is that we are losing nature faster than it can restore itself and this may mean mass extinction.

Chryssa Velissariou

Of course, there are conventions and networks like The Emerald Network, The New Deal, Global Biodiversity Framework, and Paris Agreement that work to preserve species, protect habitats, restore nature, and end poverty and hunger. A total war can destroy everything.

Moreover, the Earth is warming up at a steady pace because of the greenhouse gases. Trees help regulate the climate by absorbing CO_2 from the atmosphere. Because of global warming, permafrost and ice melting massively at the poles can increase the sea level and cause natural disasters like floods, hurricanes, storms, and wildfires. These changes are serious reasons for the population to migrate. So much ice is melting that Earth's crust is moving and the ground deforms.

In this context, the war accelerates the process.

I want to end with some lines from a poem of mine entitled Spring (Double Rondelet Triolet) :

"The red flowers bloom in the Spring

When the time for the green grass comes.

The sky vibrates like a bass string.

The red flowers bloom in the Spring.

I see nature's purest swing.

The wind searches his bongo drums,

The red flowers bloom in the Spring

When the time for the green grass comes.

I see His love

Like a white lily among thorns.

100 SENRYU AGAINST WW3

I see His love

Like in clefts of the rock, a dove.

When a red flower its grass adorns

And her dead Winter, Spring mourns,

I see His love. "

Chryssa Velissariou

100 SENRYU AGAINST WW3

1. Darkness in your eyes
    Rejection's terror
    Pale virgin lilies

2. Because of this war
    This year's blooming Spring
    Mass graves' ornament

100 SENRYU AGAINST WW3

Chryssa Velissariou

3. How can you fathom
    Nuclear weapons fights?
    You're not God, are you?

4. Don't dare to mutate
    Even a wild bud's beauty...
    Or you're just the Beast!

5. How could a poet
    Not feel disgusted by such
    A distorted war?

6. His soul would be idle
    Not considering this as
    Social distortion

Chryssa Velissariou

I HATE WAR!

7. TV omens are
    Predators of the evil
    That is still to come

8. I often wonder
    Who could be persuaded
    By spurious causes?

9. Hypnotized people
    Behind terrifying masks
    Become best herd

10. Let us try once more
    Be vaccinated against
    The-true-cause virus!

100 SENRYU AGAINST WW3

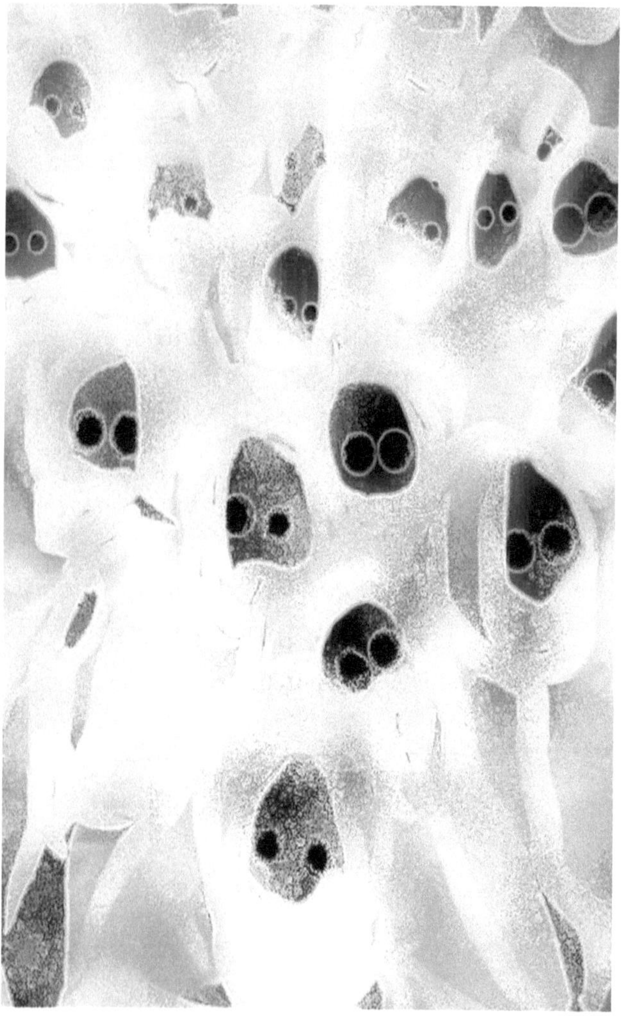

Chryssa Velissariou

11. Europe's sad women
    Get down the streets dressed
    in black / Scarecrows to evil

12. Dawn for a walk
    The dead flowers' aroma
    Coming from the North

Chryssa Velissariou

13. Ukraine Skull place
    Plague, famine, climate
    change / Who says "NO"?

14. Victory's a lie
    What would be your actual
    gain? / Just stop the war!

15. Who's winning the war?
    Whose interest is augmented
    Human trafficking!

16. One thing I'm sure of:
    Humans are not civilized
    Their true culture's hate!

Chryssa Velissariou

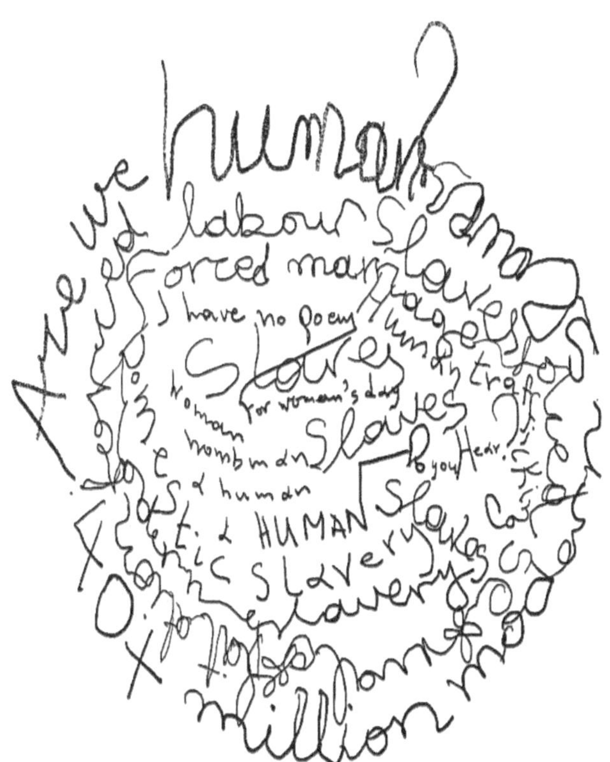

17. The TV voyeur
    Is also a warmonger
    He fakes he doesn't see

18. How many reacted?
    None pawn their secure
    comfort / Their own nirvana!

Chryssa Velissariou

19. Peace is far away
    Damage to Nature became
    Irreversible

20. We are sitting there
    In front of the tele-box
    Evading the truth

21. Some rub their hands in glee
    Because tender flesh's flowing
    For exploitation

22. X to quarrels, no?
    Only love, is it possible?
    Repeat I clichés?

Chryssa Velissariou

23. I thought that you are
    The end but the End
    Is like Babushka

24. I never believed,
    Hydra, you got beaten
    By Hercules fire

Chryssa Velissariou

25. Oh Life! You grow
    Like the wild flower beneath
    Pavement's cement

26. Well, my dear ladies,
    How do we win a war? Ha!
    Through the sprouts' harvest…

100 SENRYU AGAINST WW3

27. I should cut my tongue
    I should tie up my hand / Not
    to showcase EU's disgrace

28. Europe united
    In the streets to demand
    NO WAR! PEACE!

29. Everywhere around
    Sunflowers and dead bodies
    For what such hatred?

30. Years of struggle against
    Environment Pollution...
    Boom and it's futile!

Chryssa Velissariou

31. No more plastic bags...
    Millions of self-tests' plastic
    Pollute the ocean!

32. Renewable sources...
    Construct a war to make it
    More profitable!

Chryssa Velissariou

33. Earth is rotating
    The actor shows off on TV
    And the lambs, chopped meat

34. Between the futile
    And the incorruptible
    Just feel and live now!

Chryssa Velissariou

35. The eyes are shining
    More than the bombs around
    Take a deep look at me!

36. Do not retreat, please!
    Our worse enemy will be
    The hovering fear

37. During war's time
Remember again that
The end is near

38. The crowds always are
The operating fuel
Of the arrogance

Chryssa Velissariou

39. And we can nothing
    Capture except for the rear
    Aroma of moments

40. Do not care for what
    Went away and what will
    come / It has no meaning

100 SENRYU AGAINST WW3

Chryssa Velissariou

41. Take a deep look at me
    Until you manage to feel
    That you exist

42. Let's give a sense to
    The fact that stars' material
    Gives our soul a form

43. Seize the beauty and
    The perpetuated dream
    Grab the baton!

44. And leave other people
    Be consumed forever in
    Meaningless disputes

Chryssa Velissariou

45. Will the birds, frightened
    By the bombs, tweet and
    flutter / With a broken heart?

46. Nothing worse than the
    Lack of remorse in front of
    Nature's rape

Chryssa Velissariou

47. The disrespect to
     The divine inclination
     Of nature's protectors

48. The mockery against
     The sensitive children who
     Fight for their future

100 SENRYU AGAINST WW3

Chryssa Velissariou

49. Old man, at death's door
    Who, hell, gives you the right
    To harm the morrow?

50. I hate to scratch on
     Your Pain and Sorrow about
     The war's slaughtering

51. EU subtle chicks are
    Not used to be thrown a hand
    Across, so we're shocked

52. No good politics
    To shut our eyes and wish this
    Nightmare to end up

Chryssa Velissariou

53. I wish to dig 'n grow
    The awareness flowers
    Their scent will save us all

54. Tomorrow, I'll fly
    On a plane; I'll feel free
    So terrified though!

100 SENRYU AGAINST WW3

Chryssa Velissariou

55. I never mind height
    I just hate Death to fly back
    Towards Ukraine

56. Dawn is coming and
    I'm thinking I leave behind
    Only deep love

57. Every quarrel
    Could be mutated through a
    Mutual consent

58. Even when passion
    And lust is rejected let
    Affection remain

Chryssa Velissariou

59. The feelings are not
    Garbage to be thrown away
    Let acceptance be built

60. The growth of warriors
    Finds its fruitful soil on the
    Cliff of arrogance

61. Let's learn to endure
    The flaws of the other like
    We endure our own

62. It's dawning and I'm
    Thinking of the only one
    Who shut me out

63. The dead-end is nailing me
    The mental abstinence aches
    A cut withered rose

64. Internal conflicts
    And impasses are digging
    Traps driving to riots

Chryssa Velissariou

65. The insecure wolves
    Mourn alone and hurt, ready
    To rush into the sheep

66. It is really strange
    Some base their common life
    On their first glance

67. Other people kill
    The meaning of a mother's life
    In the blink of an eye

68. Ocean seems very
    Calm at West Europe's end
    On the east Death reigns

100 SENRYU AGAINST WW3

Chryssa Velissariou

69. I didn't forget it
    I'm just speechless cos others
    Keep forgetting it

70. The ocean keeps still
    It's holding itself calm;" No
    Bad example", it says

71. Around the world, one
    Hundred friends applaud or
    not / Putin; Is there war?

72. For me no matter
    What; I just wish the birds to
    Fly completely free

Chryssa Velissariou

73. Killed dogs, cats, cattle, sheep
    Slaughtered foxes, badgers
    Shot squirrels, weasels

74. There are also men
    Who know the situation
    But they could not fly

Chryssa Velissariou

75. Out on a terrace
    In Lisbon, Portugal
    Thinking of the world

76. Some birds are chirping
    Some greenery is growing
    A noise of construction

77. The ocean wondering
    The population of Europe
    A turbulent wave

78. A woman on the edge
    Fighting ancient monsters
    Crawling out of myths

79. Conquerors fainted
    In the depths of history
    But blood keeps flowing

80. I'm suspicious and
    Angry because human race
    Continues gold's quest

81. Why haven't we improved?
    Will love and peace ever
    reign? / Evolution sucks

82. Three hours before my
    Flight to heaven I'm informed
    I'll pass through hell

Chryssa Velissariou

83. I worked all my life
    For this damn trip! I don't care
    If I'm going to lose

84. But hell! I don't trust
    The pilot neither the crew
    They like fire and snakes!

E.U.

Chryssa Velissariou

85. Three hours before my
    Flight, I doubt if I'll avoid
    My dark destiny

86. Fearful are the wars
    That everybody is used
    To their existence

87. I'm afraid of wars
    Smoldering insidiously
    During centuries

88. Wars silent killers
    Which give birth to violent
    bursts / And nurture deep hate

Chryssa Velissariou

89. Wars with enslaved people
    In never ending quarrels
    Tragic fade's shadows

90. "War goes always with
    Trade and no rich trade exists
    When peace reigns", he stated

91. Shhh! Please talk about
    Sardines and wines, anything
    Makes you feel happy

92. Eurovision, yes!
    Console the dead people
    In Ukraine with songs...

93. The "good" ones receive
    A prize and the "evil" ones...
    Let them burn in Hell!

94. In the meantime, though
    The arms' and ammunitions'
    Big business's thriving!

95. Are one hundred senryu
    Enough to protest against
    The loss of world peace?

96. Violence and hate
    Mass graves, inhumanity
    And silent corpses

Chryssa Velissariou

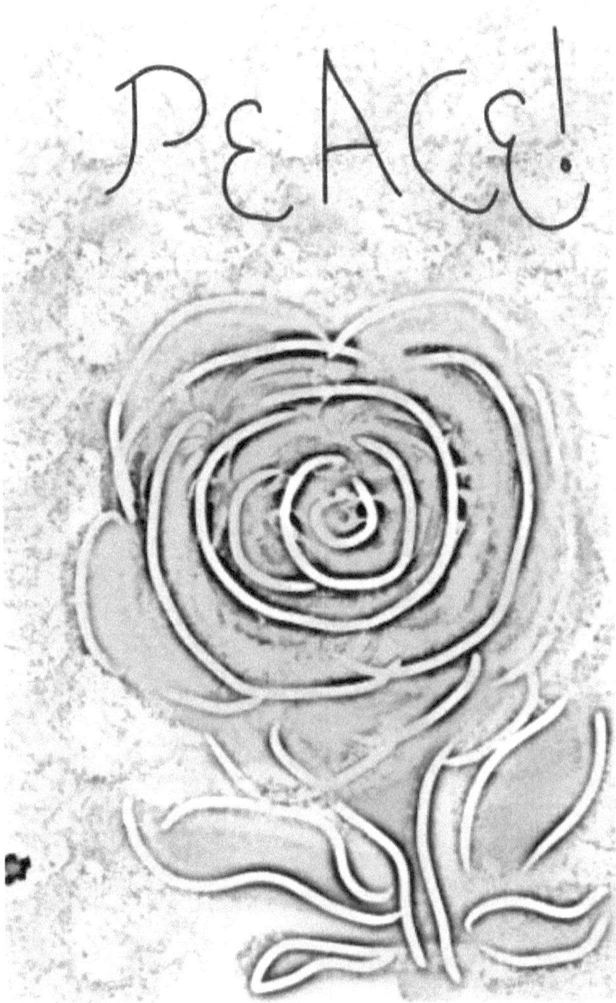

97. Bad omens, curses
    War crimes and imperialism
    A foggy future

98. Can one hundred poems
    Mourn and console the wise
    Ones / While Evil prevails?

99. Endless useless words
Rhetoric that runs out
When a mine explodes

100. Just after the plague
We take out each other's
eyes / What a paranoia!

100 SENRYU AGAINST WW3

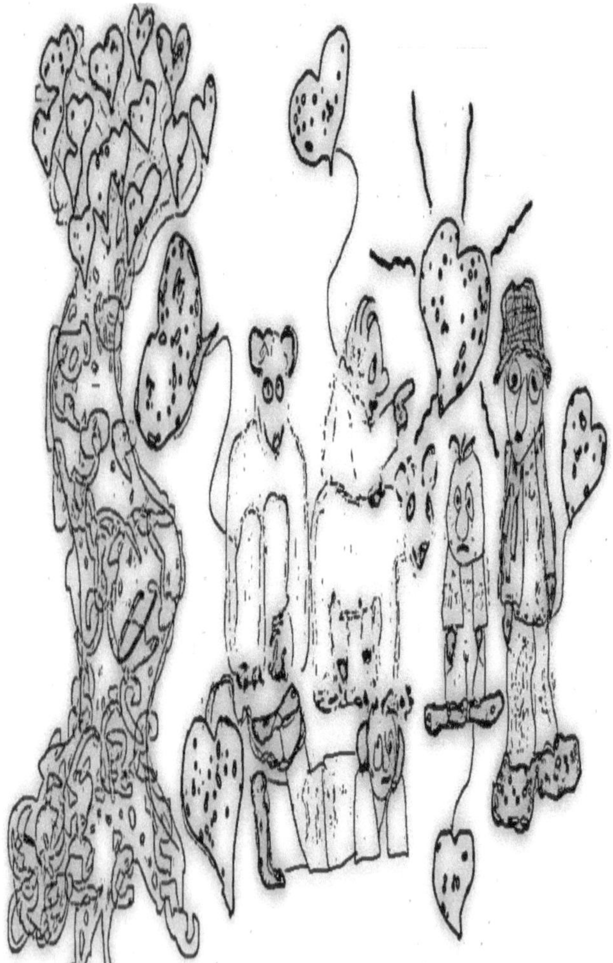

Chryssa Velissariou

Instead of an epilogue

A comment on the recent Greek-Turkish disputes

1. Not about the war!
    Let's talk only about Peace!
    Let's spread awareness!

2. Praise the best for all!
    Let's invite both peoples to
    Create the future!

3. What is wiser than
    To be ok with our neighbor!
    There's no gain in hate

4. Let's all enjoy Wealth
    And Love, the Peace's fruits;
    Here's how we'll prevail!

5. Or will the vultures
    Be the benefited ones
    Fed with our corpses?

6. Oh, be vigilant!
    Keep at least one eye open!
    Don't become their prey!

Chryssa Velissariou

100 SENRYU AGAINST WW3